Little Wild Horse Canyon

Howling wind swirls, gusts push us
along the way
into
Little Wild Horse Canyon

Wild, natural energy
forms the canyon
nature's ability to sculpt
our world

Our personal wind
breath
full of zest
shapes our life

Breathe
open self, relax
allow breath's force to align your body
breath sculpts us

Gently guide breath
from navel area
send breath into spine
feel firm support of back

New ease
enjoy breath
direct breath's pressure
rise along the spine

Gently press breath out to
expand chest
softly fill body
breath opens new insights

Smile with exhale
floating smile into body
sensing & merging
earth's support

Feel
self guided breath stretch us
align, allow
fullness of body

enjoy relaxation
breath aligns posture, kneads pain gently
such conscious attention
opens consciousness widely

Harmony
develops with persistent
alignment of ease within
breath sparks awareness throughout our being

Breath supports me

frees my Spirit

empowers

Vision, humor

A wild horse
moves our body
intuition & mind
offer guidance

My wild powerful horse
feels my breath's subtle nurturance
drinks balanced energy
released by my directed breath

Superb horse
grows into new fullness
united flow
moves with robust ease

Oh, great horse
empowered by mindful breath
within our canyon body
carry me

Through life
with patient love
joyous exploration
into harmonious fulfillment

Notes

Other books by John Cardano

THE FABRIC OF HEALTH

The Fabric of Health is a venture to express the dimensions that weave life. Mind, spirit, and body are all involved.

NATURAL RELATIONS

Natural Relations is a picture book for all ages. Nature gives vitality to our body, mind and spirit. The benefits from nature are immeasurable.

Sometimes, I can feel as though I am alone in a wilderness. A breath changes that. I feel the touch of a breath's support within me. As I give myself attention with breath's gentle effort, breath enlivens my personal world stretching me, offering alignment and a fuller connection with life. In such a moment, I am not alone, I am united with my natural world. Breath is always available to fill and lift me into new pleasure, peace, and connectedness.

Health & Wellbeing,
John W. Cardano

Print information available on the last page

Rev. date: 12/21/2015

To order additional copies of this book, contact:
Xlibris
1-888-795-4274
www.Xlibris.com
Orders@Xlibris.com

Printed in the United States
By Bookmasters